Accelerated Reader Information
as provided by www.arbookfind.com

Interest Level (suggested maturity level):
LG (early elementary grades)

Book Level: **1.8**   AR Test: **0.5** pts.

LG - 1.8 - 0.5

DEMCO

June

By Robyn Brode

Reading Consultant: Linda Cornwell,
Literacy Connections Consulting

WEEKLY READER®
PUBLISHING

Please visit our web site at **www.garethstevens.com**.
For a free catalog describing our list of high-quality books, call 1-800-542-2595 (USA)
or 1-800-387-3178 (Canada). Our fax: 1-877-542-2596

Library of Congress Cataloging-in-Publication Data
Brode, Robyn.
   June / by Robyn Brode ; reading consultant, Linda Cornwell.
      p. cm. — (Months of the year)
   Includes bibliographical references and index.
   ISBN-10: 1-4339-1922-2   ISBN-13: 978-1-4339-1922-0 (lib. bdg)
   ISBN-10: 1-4339-2099-9   ISBN-13: 978-1-4339-2099-8 (softcover)
   1. June (Month)—Juvenile literature.   2. Holidays—United States—Juvenile literature.
   3. Vacations—United States—Juvenile literature.   I. Cornwell, Linda.   II. Title.
   GT4803.B768   2010
   398'.33—dc22   2008055889

This edition first published in 2010 by
Weekly Reader® Books
An Imprint of Gareth Stevens Publishing
1 Reader's Digest Road
Pleasantville, NY 10570-7000 USA

Copyright © 2010 by Gareth Stevens, Inc.

Executive Managing Editor: Lisa M. Herrington
Senior Editors: Barbara Bakowski, Jennifer Magid-Schiller
Designer: Jennifer Ryder-Talbot

Photo Credits: Cover, back cover, title © SW Productions/Getty Images; p. 7 © Masterfile; p. 9
© Bobbi Lane/Weekly Reader; pp. 11, 17, 19, 21 © Ariel Skelley/Weekly Reader; p. 13 © Blend
Images Photography/Veer; p. 15 © Ryan McVay/Getty Images

Printed in the United States of America

1 2 3 4 5 6 7 8 9 10 11 10 09

Table of Contents

Welcome to June! 4

Special Days 12

School Is Out! 16

Glossary 22

For More Information 23

Index 24

Boldface words appear in the glossary.

Welcome to June!

June is the sixth month of the year. June has 30 days.

Months of the Year

Month	Number of Days
1 January	31
2 February	28 or 29*
3 March	31
4 April	30
5 May	31
6 June	**30**
7 July	31
8 August	31
9 September	30
10 October	31
11 November	30
12 December	31

*February has an extra day every fourth year.

In June, spring ends and **summer** begins. Summer begins on June 20 or 21.

The first day of summer is the longest day of the year. It has more hours of sunlight than any other day.

In many places, June is warm and sunny. Sunshine helps plants and flowers grow.

 What kinds of flowers grow where you live?

flowers

Special Days

June 14 is **Flag Day**. On that day, Americans honor our country's flag.

The third Sunday in June is Father's Day. Kids give cards and gifts to dads and other men who are important to them.

School Is Out!

In some places, school ends in June. Summer **vacation** begins.

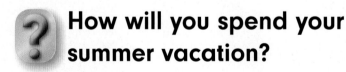 **How will you spend your summer vacation?**

Many friends have fun at the playground in summer.

playground

When June ends, it is time for July to begin.

Glossary

Flag Day: a day to honor the American flag, celebrated on June 14

summer: the season between spring and fall, when the weather is the warmest of the year

vacation: time away from school or work

For More Information

Books

My Dad. Meet the Family (series). Mary Auld (Gareth Stevens Publishing, 2004)

The Playground. I Like to Visit (series). Jacqueline Laks Gorman (Gareth Stevens Publishing, 2005)

Web Sites

Father's Day Games and Activities
www.apples4theteacher.com/holidays/fathers-day
Find poems about dads, games, and coloring pages.

Flag Day
www.enchantedlearning.com/crafts/flagday
Make red, white, and blue crafts.

Index

daylight 8

Father's Day 14

Flag Day 12

flowers 10

playground 18

school 16

vacation 16

weather 10

About the Author

Robyn Brode has been a teacher, a writer, and an editor in the book publishing field for many years. She earned a bachelor's degree in English literature from the University of California, Berkeley.